THE ULTIMATE
Hippo
BOOK FOR KIDS

100+ Amazing Hippo Facts, Photos, Quiz + More

Jenny Kellett

MELBOURNE · SOFIA · BERLIN

Copyright © 2023 by Jenny Kellett

Hippos: The Ultimate Hippo Book for Kids
www.bellanovabooks.com

All rights reserved. No part of this book may be reproduced in any form by any electronic or mechanical means including photocopying, recording, or information storage and retrieval without permission in writing from the author.

ISBN: 978-619-264-000-2
Imprint: Bellanova Books

Contents

Introduction 4
Hippos - The Basics 7
Characteristics 14
Their Daily Lives 26
Subspecies of hippos 43
    Great Northern Hippo 44
    East African Hippo 46
    Cape Hippo 48
    West African Hippo 50
    Angola Hippo 50
    Pygmy Hippopotamus 52
From Birth to Adulthood 56
Hippos and Humans 68
Hippo Quiz 80
    Answers 84
Word search 86
Sources 89

Introduction

Hippopotamuses may have one of the hardest names to spell in the animal kingdom, but they are also incredibly fascinating creatures. Their large, stocky bodies and cartoon-like features have made them a favourite among animal lovers. But despite looking adorable, they are one of the world's most dangerous animals!

So are you ready to learn more about the so-called "river horse"? *Let's go!*

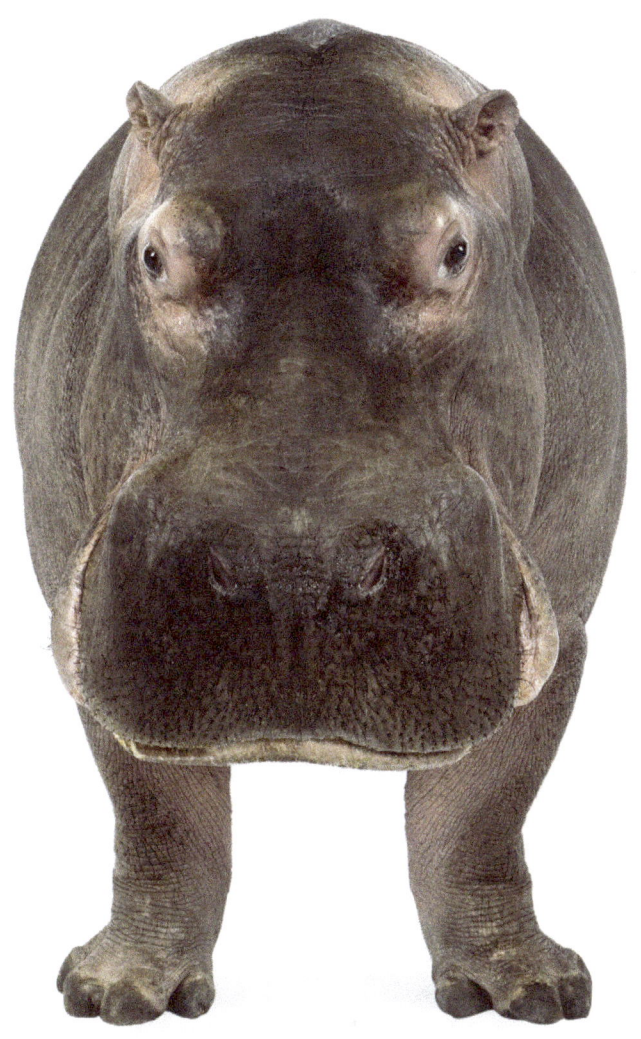

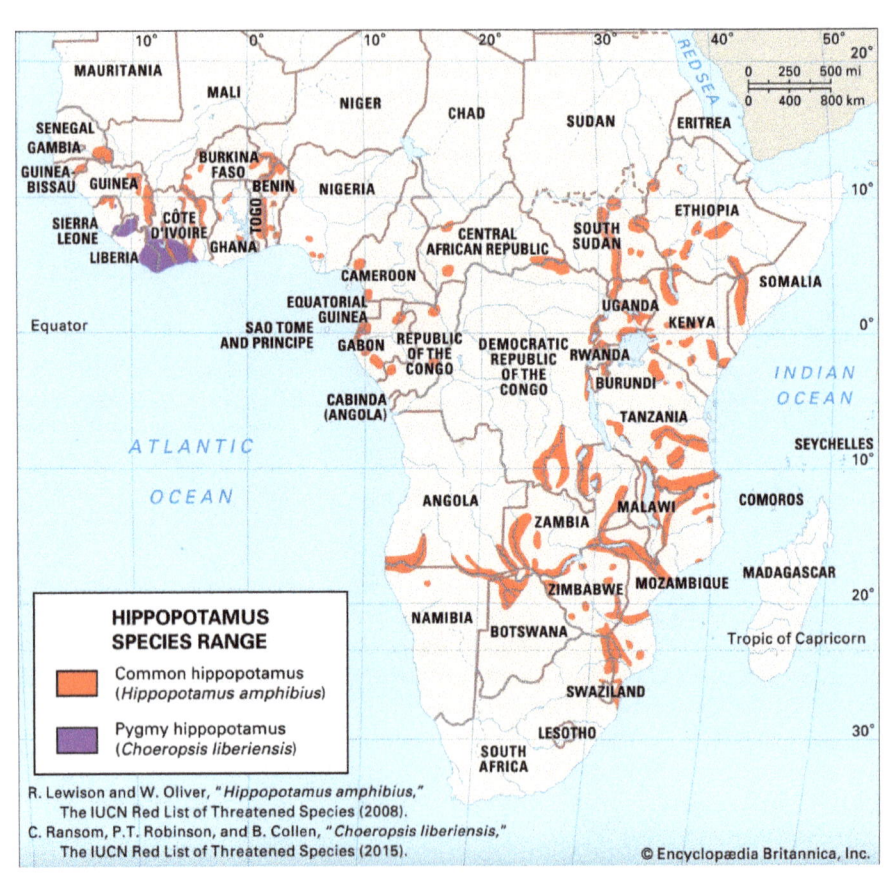

Credit: Encyclopedia Britannica.

HIPPOS:
THE BASICS

What are hippos and where do they live?

Hippopotamuses (or hippos) live in sub-Saharan Africa.

• • •

The word hippopotamus comes from the Ancient Greek word meaning **'horse of the river'**.

• • •

Hippos are the third-largest land mammals globally, after elephants and white rhinos.

The scientific name for the hippo is *hippopotamus amphibius*. There are five subspecies within the hippopotamus amphibius species, which we'll look at later on.

• • •

Hippos belong to the family **hippopotamidae**, which also includes the pygmy hippopotamus.

• • •

Until 1909, naturalists put hippopotamuses in the same group as pigs as they had similar teeth. However, we now known that the hippo's closest living relatives are actually whales and dolphins.

Hippos like to live in wet areas such as mangroves, swamps and around rivers and lakes.

• • •

There was a time when hippos were a common sight across Europe and Asia. However, due to climate change and hunting they haven't been seen in these regions since around 11,700 years ago.

• • •

Thanks to their enormous size, hippos help to create micro-habitats for smaller organisms. For example, fish often feed off the algae on the hippo's skin.

The lifespan of a hippo is about 40 years in the wild and 50 years in captivity. They live longer in captivity because trained keepers are able to monitor their health, provide them with the exact nutrition they need and keep them safe from danger.

• • •

Female hippos are called **cows**, and the males are called **bulls**.

• • •

There used to be another species of hippo called the **Malagasy hippo**. It lived in Madagascar and was smaller than today's hippos. However, it became extinct around 1,000 years ago due to hunting by humans.

A hippo's habitat is critical. The water needs to be deep enough for them to be fully submerged, although not too deep as they can't float or swim, and enough grass must surround it for them to eat.

• • •

Hippos generally live in freshwater, but West African populations often live in saltwater estuaries.

HIPPOPOTAMUS CHARACTERISTICS

Size, features, special traits and more.

Don't try to lift a hippo! A male hippo weighs an average of 1,500 kg (3,310 lb), and the females weigh 1,300 kg (2,870 lb). The largest hippo ever recorded was at a zoo in Germany: he weighed 4,490 kg (9,900 lb)!

• • •

Hippos have grey to muddy-brown coloured skin, which fades to a pink colour underneath.

A hippo running.

Hippos are enormous, ranging from 1.8-4.9 metres (6-16 ft) long. They are around 1.4 m (4.6 ft) tall to the shoulder.

• • •

Despite having short legs and stocky bodies, hippos can run 30 km/h (19 mph) over short distances! That's as fast as a human.

• • •

Hippos are **herbivores**, meaning they only eat plants. For their size, hippos don't eat a lot of food. They only need around 36 kg (80 lb) per day as most of the time they are buoyed in the water, which means they use much less energy than animals that walk on land.

Although hippos aren't fussy eaters, they generally don't eat aquatic plants. Their favourite food is short grass.

• • •

It's always a good idea to wear sunblock, even if you're a hippo! However, hippos produce their own natural sunblock: a red, oily liquid protecting them from dangerous UV rays. This liquid, which is largely a mystery to biologists, also keeps their skin moist and protects against bacterial infections.

Hippos have very dense bones, which help them easily sink to the water's bottom.

• • •

Compared to other animals their size, hippos have very short legs. However, this isn't a problem for them. Have you noticed how you feel lighter in water? It is the same for hippos—so they don't need long legs to carry their enormous weight.

• • •

Hippos can't jump, but they can climb up steep terrain like river banks.

If you look at a hippo, you'll see its eyes, nose and ears are close to the top of their heads. This allows them to keep most of their body underwater but still be able to see, smell and hear their surroundings.

...

Hippos are semi-aquatic, meaning they live partially in the water. However, despite having webbed feet, hippos can't swim very well or even float. So, a hippo in deep water will jump between spots rather than swim.

The hippo's jaw joint sits far back in its mouth, meaning it can open its mouth at nearly 180°. When its mouth is open, it is half a metre wide!

• • •

Hippos' teeth sharpen themselves as they grind their teeth. This is important as their teeth never stop growing.

• • •

A hippo's incisor teeth can reach 40 cm (1 ft 4 in), and their molars are even bigger: up to 50 cm (1 ft 8 in)!

Despite having such huge teeth, hippos don't use them for eating—only for fighting.

• • •

Hippos have very little hair, which is unusual for semi-aquatic animals.

• • •

Hippos can fold their ears and nostrils shut when they go underwater to keep out water.

• • •

Hippos' skin is 6 cm (2 in) thick, which gives them a great defence against predators.

HIPPOS
DAILY LIVES

What do hippos do all day?!

It gets scorchingly hot in Africa, so hippos spend most of their days in the water or mud to help stay cool and hydrated.

• • •

After dusk, hippos emerge from the water to graze on grass—often until the morning.

A hippo enjoying its favourite meal: short grass.

Hippos may walk up to 10 km (6 miles) each evening to search for food. When they find it, they will graze for five to six hours.

• • •

Hippos like to spend time together in the water but prefer grazing alone.

• • •

Hippos like to huddle together in the water, but scientists aren't sure why as they don't form social bonds like other animals.

A large pod of hippopotamuses.

Hippos live in **pods** or **herds**. There are between 5 and 100 hippos in a pod, including bulls, cows and calves. Within the pods, there are smaller groups, usually separated by gender.

• • •

Hippos aren't territorial when they are on land, but it's completely different when they're in the water. The main bull will keep watch over an area of water, usually around 250 m (270 yd) in length.

• • •

Hippos' poop is full of nutrients, which is an essential part of the food chain.

Not many animals try to mess with hippos as they are so huge! Hippos live in harmony with other animals most of the time. However, small and young hippos may be preyed upon by lions, spotted hyenas and Nile crocodiles.

• • •

The territorial bull in a pod is called the "beachmaster". He spends most of his time alone.

Hippos can hold their breath underwater for up to five minutes! They will often use this time to walk along the river or lake bed.

• • •

Hippos can tell the difference between a friend and a foe by smelling their dung (poop).

• • •

Like several other species, hippos often poop in **middens**—specific areas where they return to do their business. They use these to mark the boundaries of their territory.

Hippos move in the water at a speed of around 8 km/h (5 mph), coming up to breathe every three to five minutes. Calves need to breathe every two to three minutes.

• • •

Hippos can sleep fully submerged in water but still come up to breathe without waking up.

• • •

Hippos use their firm lips to grab and pull up grasses, rather than using their teeth.

If hippos spend too long outside of the water, their skin starts to crack. So it's important that they keep themselves moist.

• • •

It might not be their most endearing behaviour, but **"muck-spreading"** is a popular activity for hippos. It involves spinning their tails while pooping to spread it as far as possible. Scientists aren't sure why they do this. Perhaps it's just fun!

• • •

Hippos are famous for their huge "yawns". These yawns are, in fact, a sign of aggression.

Hippos can be very noisy. The most common noise you'll hear them make is called a **"wheeze honk"**; it sounds like a high-pitched squeal followed by a lower sound and can be heard over long distances.

• • •

One of the hippo's party tricks is holding its head half above and half under the water and letting out a sound that animals can hear in and out of the water.

During the dry season, as many as 150 hippos share a small water area. It can get very crowded!

• • •

When there is a drought, hippos may have to walk long distances to find water, which can be very dangerous. Sadly, many don't survive the journey.

• • •

Although you will often see hippos basking in the sun, they can dehydrate very quickly, so they must go for regular dips in the water.

Hippos enjoying the sunshine.

HIPPOS: SUBSPECIES

There are five **subspecies** of hippopotamus. However, the differences between them are very small and so many scientists don't recognise them as different species. They are mostly told apart based on where they live.

Let's take a look to see the differences!

GREAT NORTHERN OR NILE HIPPOPOTAMUS

Hippopotamus amphibius Amphibius

The Great Northern hippo is also known as the **common hippo**. It is the hippo you are most likely to see in a zoo or in the wild. They used to live across Egypt, hence the name, but they became extanct there in the 1800s.

Even earlier, however, the Great Northern hippopotamus freely roamed in Europe and Asia. A wonderfully intact fossil of this subspecies was found in Great Britain. Now, they can only be found along the Nile River in Tanzania and Mozambique where they like to live in deep riverbeds.

EAST AFRICAN HIPPOPOTAMUS

Hippopotamus amphibius Kiboko

The East African hippopotamus is found in Kenya's African Great Lakes region and Somalia.

The best way to recognise them is by their slightly wider nostrils than the Great Northern hippo.

Herd of East African hippopotamuses in Mara river, Masai Mara National Park, Kenya. >

CAPE OR SOUTH AFRICAN HIPPO

Hippopotamus amphibius capensis

The Cape or South African hippopotamus lives in southern Africa from Zambia down to South Africa. Out of all the subspecies, it has the most flattened skull.

Cape hippos used to be very widespread, but now they are only found in smaller areas. Many live in partial captivity, such as in national parks and nature reserves.

WEST AFRICAN OR TCHAD HIPPO

Hippopotamus amphibius tschadensis

As the name suggests, West African hippopotamuses live in West Africa. They have a slightly shorter and broader face than other species. They also have huge nostrils.

ANGOLA HIPPO

Hippopotamus amphibius constrictus

The Angola hippopotamus lives in Angola, the southern Democratic Republic of Congo and Namibia. Their main physical difference is also in the nostrils! They are deeper than the other subspecies.

Common hippopotamus in Botswana.

PYGMY HIPPO
Choeropsis liberiensis

The pygmy hippopotamus is the only other species in the *hippopotamidae* family. So are they just small hippos? Let's find out.

The pygmy hippopotamus lives in West Africa's forests; most live in Liberia, but there are also smaller populations in Sierra Leone, Ivory Coast, and Guinea. Sadly, pygmy hippos are rare in the wild—only around 2,500 exist today. Fortunately, they breed very well in captivity, which is great news for their future.

In terms of form, pygmy hippos are very similar to common hippos, but they are only about half the size. The main differences between the two subspecies lie in their behaviour.

Pygmy hippos are much less aggressive, and if there is a meeting, they tend to ignore each other rather than pick a fight. They are timid and prefer to live alone or in very small groups.

The main threat to the pygmy hippo is **habitat loss**. Many of the forests that pygmy hippos like to live in are logged to make way for different types of agriculture. In Liberia, pygmy hippos are also hunted for meat.

Like the common hippo, pygmy hippos don't have many natural predators, although as they are smaller, they are more likely to be attacked by leopards, crocodiles, and large snakes.

FROM BIRTH TO ADULTHOOD

Baby hippos are some of the cutest in the animal world, so let's learn more about their early life.

Hippos *really* do love the water. They mate and (usually) give birth in the water.

• • •

When a cow gives birth she only has around 40 seconds to get her calf up to the surface to have its first breath.

Baby hippos are called **calves**.

∙ ∙ ∙

Cows can start breeding at around five years old; bulls start at about 7.5 years old. However, hippos in captivity often begin breeding as young as three years old.

∙ ∙ ∙

Hippos prefer to mate at the end of the wet season (summer), meaning most calves are born at the beginning of the next wet season (winter).

The hippos' **gestation period** (how long a female is pregnant) is 243 days or eight months. Pygmy hippos' is slightly shorter: six to seven months.

• • •

Cows and calves have a very strong bond—this is the benefit of being an only child! They nuzzle, groom and cuddle with each other.

• • •

When calves are born, they weigh between 13-22 kg (30-50 lb). However, pygmy hippos don't weigh much more than human babies.

After a cow gives birth, she will isolate herself for 10-14 days before she feels safe enough to return to her pod.

• • •

Female hippos usually give birth every two years.

• • •

Cows usually only give birth to one calf, but twins can happen occasionally.

As hippos are **mammals**, their young drink milk from their mothers. When the water is too deep for them, they will rest on their mother's back but swim underwater to suckle.

• • •

Calves will usually suckle until they are one year old but start to eat grass when they are six to eight months old.

• • •

When calves are born, they join a **'school'** with their mother to protect them from predators such as crocodiles.

Hippo calves can float before they can walk.

• • •

Scientists believe that male hippos keep growing their entire lives, while females are fully developed at around 25 years old.

• • •

Calves stay with their mothers for a few years, often gaining some siblings along the way.

• • •

In 2017, zookeepers were able to take the first ever ultrasound image of a pregnant hippo. Normally this is impossible to do as hippos are so hard to train.

A hippopotamus family in Namibia.

HIPPOS AND HUMANS

We may be very different, but we all share the same planet.

Hippos and humans have been interacting for thousands of years. Rock paintings and engravings featuring hippos from over 4,000 years ago were found in the Sahara desert.

· · ·

Hippos are often called **'river horses'**.

Despite their calm demeanour, hippos are one of the most dangerous animals in the world. They are very territorial and can be highly unpredictable.

• • •

Hippos have been known to bite canoes in half and attack humans—often mistaking them for crocodiles.

• • •

Sadly, hippos are threatened by habitat loss. They are also hunted for their meat and ivory teeth.

The demand for hippo ivory increased after 1989, when elephant ivory was banned worldwide.

• • •

In the 19th century, hippo ivory was commonly used to make false teeth.

• • •

The **IUCN Red List** lists hippos as **vulnerable**. This means that they are close to extinction, and it is essential that we protect them.

Hippos are a popular exhibit at zoos around the world. When they are well cared for, they generally live longer in captivity than in the wild.

• • •

Bertha the hippo is the oldest known hippo kept in captivity—she lived at Manila Zoo in the Philippines until the age of 65.

• • •

The first known hippo to be kept in captivity was in Hierakonopolis, Egypt, in 3500 BC. In modern times, the first zoo to have a resident hippo was London Zoo when Obaysch arrived on 25 May 1850. He attracted over 10,000 visitors a day.

A hippo photographed underwater at Busch Gardens Zoo, Florida.

The worst decline in hippo populations is in the Democratic Republic of Congo. In the 1970s, the hippo population in Virunga National Park was estimated at 29,000; by 2005, this number was 800-900. This is because there was less focus on stopping poachers from killing hippos during the Second Congo War. Numbers, fortunately, are now increasing.

• • •

In the 1970s, Pablo Escobar—a famous Colombian criminal—kept four hippos in his private **menagerie** (personal zoo). After his death, they were left to roam free, and now over 100 hippos are living in Colombia.

Hippos were almost introduced to the USA! In 1910, a senator in Louisiana tried to pass the "American Hippo Bill" to bring hippos to the state. President Theodore Roosevelt backed the bill, but it narrowly missed out on being passed.

• • •

There are lots of famous fictional hippos. The movies *Madagascar, Fantasia* and *Hugo the Hippo* are just some that feature a hippo. Which ones have you seen?

• • •

The plural of hippopotamus is **hippopotamuses**, although hippopotami is also sometimes used.

Hungry Hungry Hippos has been a popular board game since the 1970s. The aim of the game is for your hippo to eat as many white balls as possible. It's great fun!

• • •

In the 1850s, there was a very popular song called the *Hippopotamus Polka*. Disney used the song as inspiration for its movie *Fantasia,* which features a hippo.

In 1953 the song *I Want a Hippopotamus for Christmas* was a huge hit for child star Gayla Peevey.

• • •

World Hippo Day is on February 15th each year. As well as celebrating these wonderful animals, it's a great day to spread awareness about the challenges hippos face.

• • •

There are many ways that you can support hippos in the wild. Organisations such as *African Wildlife Foundation*, *Worldwide Fund for Nature,* and the *Turgwe Hippo Trust* all have ways for you to donate money or adopt a hippo.

HIPPO *quiz*

Now test your knowledge in our Hippo Quiz! Answers are on page 83.

1 Where do hippos live in the wild?

2 What are the hippo's closest living relatives?

3 Hippos used to live in Europe. True or false?

4 What are female and male hippos called?

5 How fast can hippos run?

6 Hippos can jump. True or false?

7 How thick is hippos' skin?

8 What are social groups of hippos called?

9 What is a beachmaster?

10 How long can hippos hold their breath for?

11 How many calves do cows usually give birth to at a time?

12 What is a hippo's gestation period?

13 How long do calves stay with their mothers for?

14 What is the hippo's main threat?

15 What was the name of the hippo who lived until 65?

16 When is World Hippo Day?

17 What is the plural of 'hippopotamus'?

18 Which South American country has a population of around 100 hippos?

19 In which country were the first captive hippos kept?

20 Pygmy hippos are more dangerous than common hippos. True or false?

ANSWERS

1. Sub-Saharan Africa.
2. Whales and dolphins.
3. True.
4. Cows (female) and bulls (male).
5. Up to 30 km/h (19 mph).
6. False.
7. 6 cm (2 in).
8. Pods or herds.
9. The territorial bull in a pod.
10. Five minutes.
11. One.
12. Eight months (243 days).
13. Several years.
14. Habitat loss.
15. Bertha.
16. February 15th.
17. Hippopotamuses or hippopotami.
18. Colombia.
19. Egypt.
20. False.

HIPPO
WORD SEARCH

A	T	V	U	L	N	E	R	A	B	L	E
G	S	U	Y	E	X	V	F	D	S	M	N
H	E	T	R	W	Z	G	B	T	J	D	U
V	M	E	H	F	S	Z	R	G	R	J	R
H	I	P	P	O	P	O	T	A	M	U	S
X	A	H	K	O	F	D	S	F	S	P	R
Z	Q	G	F	D	D	V	C	R	F	S	S
S	U	H	F	D	S	S	V	I	N	P	B
C	A	G	G	C	Q	F	C	C	B	V	F
N	T	F	S	M	A	M	M	A	L	S	D
H	I	R	E	W	A	L	V	C	X	Z	Z
F	C	P	U	Y	T	R	F	V	C	X	Z

Can you find all the words below in the word search puzzle on the left?

HIPPOPOTAMUS   GRASS   CALF

AFRICA   MAMMALS   PYGMY

SEMIAQUATIC   VULNERABLE   PODS

WORD SEARCH SOLUTION

		V	U	L	N	E	R	A	B	L	E
	S										
	E				G						
	M					R					
H	I	P	P	O	P	O	T	A	M	U	S
	A			O				F	S		
	Q				D			R		S	
	U				S			I			
	A			C				C			
	T		M	A	M	M	A	L	S		
	I				L						
	C					F					

SOURCES

10 Interesting Facts to Know About Hippos (2022). Available at: https://www.worldanimalprotection.us/blogs/10-interesting-facts-know-about-hippos (Accessed: 29 March 2022).

What's The Cleverest Thing A Hippo Can Do? (2022). Available at: https://www.vpr.org/podcast/but-why-a-podcast-for-curious-kids/2021-07-16/whats-the-cleverest-thing-a-hippo-can-do (Accessed: 29 March 2022).

hippopotamus - Pygmy hippopotamus (2022). Available at: https://www.britannica.com/animal/hippopotamus-mammal-species/Pygmy-hippopotamus (Accessed: 30 March 2022).

Nile Hippopotamus | San Francisco Zoo & Gardens (2021). Available at: https://www.sfzoo.org/nile-hippopotamus/ (Accessed: 30 March 2022).

Pygmy hippopotamus - Wikipedia (2022). Available at: https://en.wikipedia.org/wiki/Pygmy_hippopotamus (Accessed: 3 April 2022).

10 Hippo Facts! - National Geographic Kids (2017). Available at: https://www.natgeokids.com/uk/discover/animals/general-animals/ten-hippo-facts/ (Accessed: 3 April 2022).

A Hippopotamus's Care of Its Babies (2022). Available at: https://animals.mom.com/hippopotamuss-care-its-babies-11416.html (Accessed: 3 April 2022).

Family, Parenting, Pet and Lifestyle Tips That Bring Us Closer Together | LittleThings.com (2022). Available at: https://littlethings.com/pets/baby-hippo-facts/3128376-10 (Accessed: 3 April 2022).

Hippopotamus (2022). Available at: https://www.awf.org/wildlife-conservation/hippopotamus (Accessed: 4 April 2022).

Hippopotamus | Species | WWF (2022). Available at: https://www.worldwildlife.org/species/hippopotamus (Accessed: 4 April 2022).

And that's all, folks!

We'd love it if you left us a review—they always make us smile, but more importantly they help other readers make better buying decisions.

Visit us at

www.bellanovabooks.com

for more fun fact books and giveaways!

CPSIA information can be obtained
at www.ICGtesting.com
Printed in the USA
BVHW062206130123
656277BV00020B/1780